Eyes in Times of War

ALI ALIZADEH is an award-winning Iranian-born Australian poet. He migrated to Australia after living through the Islamic Revolution and the Iran–Iraq War, and is a writer of poetry, criticism and plays. The major themes of his works are history, dissent and the dilemmas of religion and spirituality. He holds a PhD in writing from Deakin University Melbourne, and this is his second book. He is currently living and teaching writing in China.

Also by Ali Alizadeh

POETRY
eliXir: a story in poetry (Grendon Press, 2002)

Eyes in Times of War

Ali Alizadeh

CAMBRIDGE

PUBLISHED BY SALT PUBLISHING
PO Box 937, Great Wilbraham, Cambridge PDO CB1 5JX United Kingdom

All rights reserved

© Ali Alizadeh, 2006

The right of Ali Alizadeh to be identified as the
author of this work has been asserted by him in accordance
with Section 77 of the Copyright, Designs and Patents Act 1988.

This book is in copyright. Subject to statutory exception
and to provisions of relevant collective licensing agreements,
no reproduction of any part may take place without the written
permission of Salt Publishing.

First published 2006

Printed and bound in the United Kingdom by Lightning Source

Typeset in Swift 9.5 / 13

*This book is sold subject to the conditions that it shall not,
by way of trade or otherwise, be lent, re-sold, hired out,
or otherwise circulated without the publisher's prior consent
in any form of binding or cover other than that in which
it is published and without a similar condition including this
condition being imposed on the subsequent purchaser.*

ISBN-13 978 1 84771 287 8 paperback
ISBN-10 1 84771 287 7 paperback

SP

1 3 5 7 9 8 6 4 2

Contents

MONSTERS — 1
- I, the Monster — 3
- War Narrative — 6
- I Am Filth — 16
- Apostasy — 18
- Your Terrorist — 21
- Happy Immigrant — 24
- The Clash — 26
- The Wind of Sheba — 30
- A Ghazal by Attar — 32

BATTLES — 35
- In Times of War — 37
- The Incinerator — 39
- Australia — 44
- France — 47
- The Opium — 50
- The Next Superpower — 53
- The Traitor — 56
- Immigration — 60
- The Honest Truth — 63

EMBERS — 65
- Rumi — 67
- Three Quatrains by Rumi — 69
- A Ghazal by Rumi — 70
- Beaten — 71
- Annihilation — 76
- A Ghazal by Attar — 79

Writer in Prison	80
Iran	82
Eyes in Times of War	86
Angelus Novus	91
Good Idea?	93
Barfly	95
The Hermit	100
This Thing	101
Golden Girl by R. Shiri	105
A Ghazal by Hafez	106
My People	107
RETROSPECT	109
Teeth in Times of War (for 8 October 2001)	111
The Ghosts (from elixir: a story in poetry)	112
ABC (from elixir: a story in poetry)	114
A Memory	126
Princess	128
The Fruiting	134
Out of Water	135
Lover's Name	136
You're the Sentinel	137
Windows #3	138

Acknowledgements

Many thanks to those who have assisted with the development of this collection and its poems: Penny Pitt-Alizadeh, Andy Jackson, Angela Costi, John Kinsella and Salt, Ken Avery, Joe De Iacovo, Matt Hetherington, Justin Clemens, Kris Terbutt, Ouyang Yu, Jess Stafford, Ashley Brown, Bill Mousoulis, Judith Rodriguez, Soraya Fuladi, Davood Alizadeh, Safoura Alizadeh and Peter Wojciechowski.

Some of the poems in this collection have been previously published in the following: *Cordite, Dan O'Connell Hotel Poems, Divan, Flaming Nibs, Going Down Swinging, Kalimat, Love & Fear, mod_piece, Red Weather, Said the Rat!, Saloni Mediterranean, Southerly, Thylazine, Verandah*, and *Writing Australia*.

Monsters

I, the Monster

I, the monster
you, the angel

are humans?
My fangs are plastic,

your wings paper;
human-made to signify

un-humanity. Such
poetry this

deformation of
reality. No, I don't

mean truth, the source
of this elaborate

fairy tale. Let the gods
play at that

as Euripides might say
'from their ethereal thrones'.

Mine is more like
a dilapidated toilet-seat

all too earthly
for the theatrics of divinity.

That makes me
monstrous? Abject?

Still too polite to say
'Can I borrow thy whitish wing

to wipe my arse?'
I play my part

in the drama of The Battle.
Such an actor

I look so defeated
toppled by your gleaming

Archangel Michael.
There. The crowds cheer

and overcome
their humanity.

Backstage I help you
slash your heavenly wrists

upon my blunted horns.
I know you'll win this war

too. I'm the archetypal
loser. At your funeral

the crowds howl louder than ever.
I'm all too indifferent

all too monstrous
to hold back my tears.

War Narrative

I.

Let's have a story, for tales
truncate the unknown and impart

wisdom. Let's say the reader
demands law and entertainment. So

let there be a hero. S/he no doubt
reflects the reader, the same

complexion as the reader, the same
lifestyle and volitions. The hero's tongue

mimics the quotidian noise
of the reader's society. Call

this fiction 'one of us', compel
identification. Reduce the tropes

of language to a common schema
of 'our values'. She is a good mother

with cute, food-loving children. He
the bread-winner with a coquettish

wife, machismo and the rest. She, of course
exceptional, parent, daughter, friend

even 'modern woman'. He displays
only the best traits of our dubious

patriarchy. But let's confine the doubts
in denial, under the surface. Let our hero/ine

cruise the surface, smile, make love
and exhibit our boundless humanity. Until

the villain comes. Now our narrative
enters initiation, development. And

the reader reaches for snacks and sniggers
with delight—Ah, what a show!

II.

Let the villain have horns, crimson eyes
and a warped voice. Best if s/he speaks

a barbaric tongue, the absolute other
of our beloved idioms. Let it not be

he or she, but part mechanical part
hermaphrodite. An insect, really, an ugly

cockroach with the mask of
humanity. It wants to steal our food,

desecrate our ideals. Watch
this abomination defecate on the clean

sites of our propriety. Look deep into
its soul and discover that, yes, it

has none. Madness becomes
our foe; not a 'mental illness' entailing cure

its opaque and sweaty lunacy. Ensure
that it gorges on things that don't

resemble (our) food. Displace 'race'
with 'culture' and rejoice in demonising

the Other by proclaiming your lack of
racism. So, yes, let our enemy be

from a 'culture' that, in contrast to ours,
means only brute 'nature'. Horns, then

can be more 'creative' metaphors. Try
beliefs that revoke ours, sexual habits

that offend our (heroes') morality. Then
show the lurid outsider's utter cruelty

its hatred of cute, food-loving children, its
violation of good mothers and 'modern

women', its affront to the might of our
no-longer dubious but now righteous

patriarchs. Let the battle begin.

III.

Does the enemy have a history?
Did it crawl out of the sewers

of pure darkness and incontestable
filth? But, more importantly,

can our tale see to questions? Would
doubt delay, even prevent

the action, the march to an exciting
confrontation? I think

I'm a party-pooper. The reader wants
rules and release, certainty

and leisure. S/he doesn't care for
pausing the drama to contemplate

the genesis of our foe's menace. What
does it matter if the enemy is not

a generic *objet d'art* but
a signifier of reality that justifies

our concept of the real, our passion
for war? I mean

doesn't the nemesis—Satan, if you like—
have parents, a past and a being

as we do? What if its horns,
knives, poisons, homemade bombs

are hollow metaphors, fake props? Our tribe
is being terrorized by scarecrows

erected by sneaky storytellers. Our enemy
only a (very demonic-looking)

costume, tailor-made for the Others?
What then? Do we still

fight, if the enemy's terror
results from ours? If its victims

are better off healed than avenged?

IV.

But we cannot have that. Only a clash
between our protagonists and 'it'.

Let's enjoy the performance, cheer for
our heroine, 'overcoming the odds'

to put on view her genius, proficiency
at, yes, love, motherhood, being 'modern',

etc. She is so unique, so unlike
the enemy. She has intellect, intuition

and an abundance of beauty. She beats
'its' innate, incurable ugliness, immorality

with stealth and (again) love. An enticing
comic resolution. The reader drools over

her competence and sexuality. Hers
the boons of contentment and rarity. The male

hero's physical power and technology
trounce the enemy. The reader leaps

with joy every time another slimy foe
incinerates in the fire of the hero's gun. If

the climax implies or explicates too much
glorious carnage then why not

a 'redemptive' denouement, say
an apologia by the dying fiend or a eulogy

by the killer-hero after the killing, even
exculpation, but only after

masculine punishment. If the enemy
is to be reformed rather than obliterated

then this correction the work
of our hero's conscience. The reader applauds

this ability to forgive the defeated
adversary. An 'ethical' finale

to the story's battle between us and evil.

V.

Can I but interrogate
our heroine's victory? Her alibi

utterly fraudulent, manufactured
by her own desires. What's to distinguish

between her 'love'
and the desires of her rival/enemy?

Why should we assume
her brilliance more palpable

than 'its'? A matter of
point-of-view? Is the reader

really that myopic? Too shallow
to object to our hero's violence

perpetrated in the name of our clan? Is
terror heroic when committed by us

and diabolical when attempted by 'it'? Who
will count the losses, timeless injuries

that outlive our story's temporality? The foe's
body and hopes are crushed. Its carcass

a site of righteousness and revenge
to indulge the reader's desperate (and denied)

lust for hatred and security. What's
to celebrate? Only upright, self-satisfied winners

and a mess of battered losers festering
in the cesspits of humiliation. Did the enemy

deserve our war? Was 'it' a threat
that called for such a horrific response? What

about justice? Are we not the very villains
who, out of a base need for survival,

clash, kill, win and gloat? Don't we deserve
'its' hatred, then, and is 'it' not a hero

who attacks our aggressive solipsism, our cruel
collective narcissism?

   VI.

Our story has been had. Now
I seek rupture from your theatres of war

to stretch out in the silent lobby. Your tales
(or the tales you'd have me tell you)

are organically belligerent, branded
'romantic', 'life-affirming' and 'inspirational'.

Your hero/ines romanticise self-righteousness,
affirm their right to take/ruin another's life

and aspire to win and destroy. I roll
on the floor and relish the chance to escape

the glow of your dazzling narrative. You
want war. I understand that. You, reader,

value triumph above justice, success
above peace. My questions annoyed you. In fact

you would've preferred watching a movie or
waging a war than being subjected to, of all things,

a poem (a long one, at that). But I don't seek
your forgiveness. Your love of war

a matter for Judgment Day, although
such a date does not exist. For once I wish

there was a God, a force that would sabotage
and thwart this story's inevitability. So keep

your credits and let me critique: this story
had logos and pathos but nothing bordering on

an ethos. The only ethical act
committed in the text, the schism at the end

and a rejection of a sequel, or the obligatory
'they lived happily ever after'.

I Am Filth

I am filth. You are right
    to hate me. Do not listen

to the mystics' warnings; hatred
    will not corrupt your logic. I'm

the source of decadence; see my
    thick beard, dark skin and turban.

Do not listen to the learned;
    civilisation *is* a Western value.

Mine is irreversible savagery.
    Haven't you received the facts

of my innumerable barbarities
    from the mouths of newsreaders,

from the pens of your columnists?
    Listen to them. They know

what's best for your morality.
    Listen to me: I'm a virus

poised to strike at your healthy body.
    Do not underestimate me. My culture

is vampiric. My icons
    zombies. Hide your daughters from

my supernatural lust. I'm the very villain
    of your gothic horror. The monstrous Muslim

concocted by the apocalyptic fetish
    of your politicians and rabble-rousers.

Listen to them. They know how
    to make hatred necessary, user-friendly.

Let their words be mightier than the scimitars
    of my legends. Do not spare a thought

for my history. I don't have one.
    Yours is the epic of discovery and triumph;

mine an illegible, fading footnote.
    Do not worry yourself with

the story of my culture being the Cradle
    of Civilisation. You shall rock

my history to the grave
    and that's all that counts. You

can afford to be hateful. Your terror
    disguised as a 'hero quest'

for security and democracy. Enjoy
    your supremacy. Let me suffer

the consequences of being an archetype
    of your Hell. Call me evil;

call me filth.

Apostasy

Troubled by the innovative
importation of the medieval term

do I, who escaped from
the Society of the Faith,

await the *jihadist* dagger
with every pore of my throat's skin?

Do I fantasise and confuse
my banal rejection of religion

for a grand rebellion? Or ask
for perspective on the barbarity

of *fatwahs* and Islamic Fundamentalism?
Perhaps. Or else

place the Faithful's mandates
in the prosaic milieu of modernity

and discern the sheer poetry
of naming a mundane contemporary being

an 'apostate'. But the 'wordplay'
doesn't end in language. In 'reality'

a Pakistani taxi-driver warned
me of the danger of defaming 'our' creed.

"If Rushdie was here
I'd kill him myself". Well

here's some fuel for the Western
haters of swarthy Others. But

this (no doubt distorted) memory
cannot serve my discourse. The murderous

will murder. The paranoid
will fear. I'm neither. Yet disturbed

by the gothic lexicon of 'my people'
am I not forced to further renounce

the validity of a religion
(a culture? an ethnicity?)

as rich and impoverished
as any other? Shall I join the confessionals

of the slaves besotted by
the Western master's superiority?

Or ask for a reform
and a 'modern' approach to Mohammed's verse?

Do I even care enough for Islam
to wish it 'improved' or 'redeemed'

in the eyes of hateful Christians who,
of course, see themselves as Progressive,

Secular, Egalitarian, etc
in spite of all the contrary evidence?

Shall I join the predictable, fearful
condemnation of 'terrorism', 'honour killing', etc

or abuse my intellect by explaining
the reasons for 'our' grievance,

and repeat the tedious mythos
of an expired pan-Islamic fantasy

(Palestinian Dispossession, Western Decadence,
Western Greed, etc)? Neither.

I shudder and marvel at
the creativity of the otherwise trite religious;

at their use of esoteric terminology
in representing frankly bland

phenomena of today's conditions.
Much more effective being an apostate,

an idolater and a heretic
than an ex-pat, a migrant, a wog

and a nobody.

Your Terrorist

You call me a barbarian.
I call you master.

You don't speak my language.
My words

noise in your ears; my poems
meaningless melodies.

Your poems
masterpieces of literature.

Your clothes
constitute fashion; your homes

architecture.
My house

the hovel your tanks levelled;
my clothes

rags. My beliefs
crushed by your technology

because I'm a barbarian.
But I must understand

your language. O master, your words
are essential to my survival. I have to

put your goggles on my eyes
to see myself,

a dangerous alien with
incomprehensible language

and innate savagery
because you're so civilised and meaningful.

You have the weapons
the tools for proving the logic

of your power. You wear clothes
that bolster your shoulders

and accentuate your height.
Me, I'm naked

and paraded as a prisoner
on your catwalks. I've been

defeated, dispossessed, and now
detained in the cages

of your metropolis. I can't remember
if I ever had my own culture

because your powerful voice
has deafened my memories. Your logic

proves I'm a primitive
at the mercy of your civilisation.

Yes, I understand
your language. I've been learning

the lexicon of my inferiority
from behind the bars. I now know

how to spell and pronounce
the terms of my slavery. Your shackles

are called Security; your war
Operation Freedom; your cluster bombs

food parcels for my children. O master,
I understand

what you want your filthy slave to be. I am
your barbarian, your terrorist;

your monster.

Happy Immigrant

Actually slime; this my substance. Don't let
the clean *syuzhet* of my presentation fool. See

but don't believe. I've been styled in the schools
of the West; a sponge that soaked the bile

of Their hubris and *mea culpa*. I received
with blatant naiveté the Good News of Truths

from Their invention of Culture to Their regret
at Their 'accidental' advent of the Holocaust. No;

the guilt is mine: utterly mine the terror afflicted
upon the Other. A little deviousness courtesy

of Aliens like me not assisting Them overcome
Their gruesome (but 'regrettable') proclivity

for sacrificing Aliens to fire. If, my professors said,
the Aliens had declared their allegiance sooner

the fires could have been avoided. Or something
to that effect. Who was I to argue against the Truth

of their justice? A dark-skinned boy with
a Semitic tongue that he bit, chewed, and eventually

spat out in the preferred form of the Master's own
mongrel dialect. That's who. Finally graduated

from the academies of salvation and submission
modernised, you might say, but really reduced

to a caricature of the Grateful Immigrant, I could not
eradicate my native Otherness but only brush it

under the spotless lingo of Survival and Success. Having
neither survived nor succeeded, I've stored the vile

venom of my untouched content for when I may
explode like one of my Muslim terrorist namesakes

in Their immaculate shopping-malls or airports
to bathe Their glittering white outfits and pink faces

in the deluge of my internal filth and horror.

The Clash

Civilisations, it's often shouted,
clash. Particularly mine

and yours. At Thermopylae
the Persians crashed

into and squashed the Spartan
infantry. At Salamis

the Athenians sank the Persian
fleet. Romans were crushed

by Parthian horsed-archers
but they later skilfully

smashed Cleopatra and took
Egypt. Then Christianity

and the destruction
of Jerusalem's temples. Yet

my religion untouched by your
god's self-sacrifice

Zoroastrian, polytheist, Jewish
and Islam: your Romanised tribes

unified in the exigent cause
of the Cross. My side took Spain.

Yours defeated the Saracens
at Poitiers. Then the Crusades. Then

the Ottomans. Scimitars clashed
chain mail, cannons fired

on muskets. Then the tanks,
the air-raids and suicide bombers.

But do I forget to tell
you about the Muslim scholars

studying Aristotle? The English
poets translating the *ghazals*

and *rubaiyats* of Persians? Or my
watching sneakily the pirated

videos of *Friday the 13th*
and *Mad Max*? Or your eating

kebabs and saving to buy
an Afghan rug? Perhaps. But my

forgetting to include
the images of exchange

in the midst of the clatter
of the chronology of hostility

proves a little more than dubious
compared to the fallacy

of classification. How did I
become Eastern and you

my Other? Vice versa? How
am I grouped? According to what

mischievous logic? Am I
shrunken to an ethnic type? But I

don't wear turban, ride camel
have never spoken Arabic or bothered

with the Koran. Your pride in
the Acropolis, Colosseum

and Westminster Abbey, frankly
nonexistent. To what cultures

do we belong? To repeat:
mine, not of sensuality

and hashish-induced lassitude, but
a love of Rimbaud

and Belgian beer. Yours, not of greed
and rationalist modernity

but baklavas and the *Book
of Thoth*. Why determine us

by the trite significance
of hair-colour and nose-shape? What

does it take to overcome the logic
of the Third Reich? But enough

questions. What use when The Answer
is being shouted and proliferates

above the murmur of my individual's
doubt.

The Wind of Sheba

The wind of Sheba
messes with the pages

of his Scripture. A tease
or an ungodly twister?

It depends on him
and the level of his attachment

taken for granted. The folly
of being ape-man, or man-ape.

As for the black queen's part
the Testament has obscured again

(or, at least, misunderstood).
It's more than curiosity

pagan royalty brings
to Solomon's temple.

Like I said
she's not a tease. It's his

lack of conviction
to leave it up to his One God

to convince the sexy enchantress
that she's wrong

to be either sexy and/or
enchanting. He used to be confident

of his own Grace—why else
would God have eased

His periodic calamities?
Well, He hasn't. She's just that;

a wind, like I said
or more accurately

a storm. For me she's torn
the spine off all testaments.

And Muhammad, Dante and Milton
won't be able to collate the pages

of His jumbled salvation
history.

A Ghazal by Attar

From Persian, with Ken Avery

Our Master awoke at the crack of dawn.
    He went from the mosque's door towards the tavern.

He went from the circle of the religious
    to the midst of the circle of infidelity.

He drank up a flagon of lees in one gulp;
    he shouted at an idol and became a wine-drinker.

As the wine of Love did its work on him
    it made him loath to the world's good and evil.

Falling and rising like a drunkard at dawn
    he went to the bazaar clutching a cup of wine.

An uproar arose from the people of Islam:
    How dare this Master become one of the infidels!

Everyone said: Why such a desertion?
    Why would such a Master commit such treason?

Their reproach made his resolve stronger.
    In his heart the people's reproach turned prickly.

The people seemed fascinated by him
    and he was surrounded by countless spectators.

With one drink such a beloved Master
    was so disgraced in the eyes of the world's people.

The dishonoured Master was fallen drunk
    until gaining a brief awareness from drunkenness.

He said: If I've got drunk it's well and good.
    The whole of humanity must do the same thing.

Whoever is drunk in this city
    gets to be courageous and reckless.

The people said: This beggar is for killing!
    This heretic's presumptions are extreme!

The Master told them: Do the deed quickly
    for this beggar declares he's a fire-worshipper.

Hundreds of thousands of lives are offered to Her,
    for whom the souls of the righteous are sacrificed.

He said this and puffed out a burning sigh
    while mounting the ladder towards the gallows.

Foreigners and citizens, women and men
    hurled and heaped stones upon him from all directions.

The Master who gave up his life in his ascension
    became intimate with the secrets of Reality.

Eternally sheltered by Union with the Friend
    he has been nourished by the Tree of Love.

These days the story of Master Hallaj
> brings happiness to the hearts of the pious.

Within the chest and the desert of the heart
> his narrative has become the guide to Attar.

Battles

In Times of War

For the Coalition of the Willing

In times of war
clocks ring out battle cries.

The digits on your watch
calculate the casualties.

The days in your diary
marked by the news of death.

Your Friday Black,
your Sunday all Bloody.

Your almanac the schedule
for attack and counter-attack.

Fresh troops fill the dates
of your corpse-riddled calendar.

It's a quarter past
the fear of being terrorised

and forty-five minutes to
the sadism of being the aggressor.

It's the afternoon
of the day that began with bombs

and around dinner-time
we'll have persecution and genocide.

At midnight
heroes become rapists

and peace-keeping
a form of mass destruction.

So let me hibernate.
I've set the alarm

for when your hourglass of war
has used up its crimson sand.

The Incinerator

I.

You, domain of debris and ash;
whose fire constructed your black towers?

In whose excited furnace fire
and fiery science dared to collude?

Which architect designed your walls
of bricks and charred human sinews?

Whose pestle crushed the bones and lives
to fashion mortar for cobblestones?

Which creator made the people the fuel
to burn as torches on coal-black nights?

Which authority sanctioned the heat
that melted nature to mould your towns?

Your proud, infernal landmarks are raised
by whom? By whose dire commandments?

II.

After Jacques Derrida

You say this is the end
of history; I sense

fresh fumes rising
from the wreckage. You say

this is not at all
a wreckage, this wonderful

destination. You note
the revolutions and the fires

naming us the victors
of the 'timeless' conflict. I feel

nothing is timeless;
humanity has always been

a victim and an effect
of time's cruelties. You point

at the palaces
erected upon the ruins, the Light

on the Hill; 'at the end
of the tunnel'. I'm suffocating

and smouldering in the furnaces
of your Kingdom. I see

there's never been
such horror, not even at the first

apocalypse when your likes saw
the Four Riders. Or was it all

a macabre fantasy? You say
you're not a fantasist but

an Enlightened observer. You cite
philosophers and scientists

and declare that you're not
a fanatic. I am an observer too

and have seen carrions extracted
from bombed ruins and charred

martyrs in urns paraded
down the streets. I've smelt

the cooked flesh of
the children devoured by the fires

of your Cold War. I find
the devastating appeal

of the scent of your hubris
utterly rancid. You repeat this

is 'the end of history'; you sport
a white armband and wave

your Cross and celebrate and expand
your Law in place of

Justice; you say civilisation's been
perfected via Christianity,

the Enlightenment and Free Market
Capitalism. Yet I stare at the infernos

of history's unstoppable
barbarities. I watch my own

skin blister and melt in the endless
flames; and I know my cells

are cinders and my words the scars
of past and present burnings; for

my presence is the chimney-pipe
where the smokes and spectres

merge above the high-rise
turrets of your fortresses

where the despised are disposed of
in the oven; and your children

grin and warm their hands
and rejoice in the 'happy ending'

of a grotesque, endless history.

III.

He fed my passport to the flames
and rubbed his hands above the fire.

His frosted fingers trembled. I
saw my breath linger like a ghost

a transient fog. It disappeared
into the night's bleak, biting air.

At our latitude, the winter's
cold stung our skin and shook our bones.

"We'll have to cross the border now
before the guards restart the watch",

he spoke as I beheld my face
crinkle amid the fading flames.

My picture, parents, date-of-birth,
my name and my nationality

were soon cinders, and I shivered
and buried my hands in my jacket.

Australia

To achieve your grand freedom
you're destined to shackle others

in perpetuity. To renounce
your heritage of imprisonment

you shall turn the Others into
criminals. Bland observation?

Perhaps, and it won't do
for signifying the grotesquerie

of banishing refugee children
to desert cages, or denying

the horror of transforming the land's
original inhabitants into persecuted

outcasts. Your exceptional malice
not a mere fact of a forlorn genesis

say, the expression of the cruelty
endured by your convict ancestors.

A flimsy explanation for the humans
now incarcerated in the dungeons

of razor-wire and self-harm. Or
for the black man beaten to death

at the Palm Island police station. No,
for once I'm not talking to history

but its outcomes. Tell me:
schadenfreude or catharsis? Revenge

most likely. Asian and Muslim
asylum seekers must reimburse

the insults your forefathers suffered
on the convict ships. The Aborigines

shall be wiped off their land since
you were exiled from yours. But

what about the termination of the White
Australia Policy, 'equal opportunity'

statutes, and your prized
multiculturalism? No cause for pride?

You tell me: you expelled
one of your citizens because of her

bronze skin, almond eyes and Filipino
accent. You still can't acknowledge

the use of smallpox as a weapon,
or poisoned flour in exterminating

the hungry and undesirable natives
during the conquest. Racism? Don't

be dull. Your unfathomable
abhorrence makes xenophobia

hide-and-seek. You seek retribution
for being born, or at least for being

raised on a desert island, rejected
from the moist and temperate

bosom of Mother England. Can't you
admit your repulsion? Must your

hate-speech be forever flawed
by laughable allusions to fairness

and openness? Do you think me so dumb
unable to fathom not only the futility

but the utter horror of freedom
without equality? Your fetish for liberty

from the rejections and Oedipal fears
make you the very destination

of Liberal Economics and Free
Market Capitalism; and a horrific jail

for the 'inferiors' who shall forever pay
the price of your unattainable release.

France

This would be a Grand
Remonstrance if I could

confuse your story with
the revolution of your nemesis.

But how could I, of all
the avid admirers of the birth

of equality, fraternity et al,
speak here of the trivial

civil war in the dull 'nation
of shopkeepers'? I couldn't

forget the romance of change
transmitted from the heart

of your vibrant culture until
I made the pilgrimage to Bastille

and was stunned. The date
14 July. The event, I'd have thought,

the commemoration of the matrix
of modern democracy. Instead

legions of riot-police besieged
the handful of leftist amateurs

waving tattered red banners as
the brazen cavalcade of tanks

and glitzy politicians sauntered
beneath the Arc de Triomphe. Whose

triumph? Certainly not history's: in
your cradle of egalitarianism

nouveau fascists bludgeon migrants
under the aegis of a government

that cages refugees. Your leaders
deny the million deaths in Algeria

with disarming simplicity. Jeanne d'Arc
now the poster-girl of the far Right;

Voltaire and Rousseau dusty names
vanishing in the vaults of le Panthéon

and a jade-green copper column
the tribute to the sacrifices of '48

fades amid the smog at the core
of the circle of cafés and boisterous traffic

in Place de la Bastille. I was
as I said, dazed by the dated presence

of your epic past. Disenchantment
wouldn't do. Traumatised by the scope

of my misguided fealty to
a mythology never deserving

my ardent, naïve devotion. A mere
crush on you, Beautiful

France, 'moveable feast', etc,
eradicated by the blood and boils

of maturity. Perhaps. But let
me expound my outrage: at this

entrance to a new Dark Ages,
(the prelude to the next World War?)

with equality utterly expired, and
slavery and chauvinist fundamentalism

the great new ideas, who
shall lead the Revolution, who

if not you?

The Opium

The Opium continues
working its putrid magic

potently, in spite of
Uncle Karl's famous diagnosis

boy-martyrs explode
for the bosoms of Heaven's *huris*

and 'intelligent design' erodes
the brains of America's school kids.

Communism a mask
for the Passions of consumerism;

Enlightenment the façade
of unrepentant superstition.

The Opium's allure
perhaps itself an inevitability

wafts in the waves of haze
in the tattered halls of history.

What historians can't
the preachers will with certitude:

the complexity of humanity
revised in the form of Bad vs. Good.

What of Voltaire,
Shelley and Marx's children?

Reality too unfathomable,
representation too benign?

Words, mere words
biblical, cryptic or emotive

redesign borders and turn
disputes into Divine Directives.

Theocracy only unpleasant
if discerned in the Other;

the leaders of 'democracy'
regulars at churches and temples.

Doubt, once again a crime
as in the Dark Ages of Abelard.

Confidence the prize
for the believers in Heaven and Hell.

Secularism the sound
of latent religious speech;

modernism the codeword
for staunch, tribal devotion.

New Ageists fool
with sacred texts and traumas

keeping the door open
for the resurgence of darkness.

Did we resume to bow
so soon after beginning to rise?

Is history really over
now that religion has usurped reality?

Or can we still envisage
Shelley's 'glorious phantom'

to emerge when the addicts
return to renouncing the Opium?

The Next Superpower

On the much-publicised full moon
festive youths and families gorge

on overpriced moon-cakes
to celebrate mid-autumn. How

very poetic. Not all that far away
the plants' wastes flow

to choke the Yangtze. I can't
appreciate the taste of the cakes,

their severe sweetness. The Chinese
cherish the stuff. This, they say,

is a beloved tradition. I can't
remember ever loving anything

resembling one. You can't finish
yours, and stroll onto the balcony

to view the fireworks. I'm worried
about the colossal dam cracking

and the River devouring this stuffy,
miasmic city. Will nature

ever know what to do with
humans? Will humans surpass words

like 'nature', 'river' and 'moon'?
The cake, I've been told, grows

every year in price. China swells
every year in wealth and power. I'm

frankly terrified of an ecological
armageddon. You seem bored with

the festivities and utterly finished
with the West. We left Australia

for an ancient culture. How
perturbed we are to discern

this country's gargantuan
industrialisation. I leer at the remnants

of the pungent cake. The West
has traded its soul for a few dollars. Will

China remember the Opium War or
keep eating the impossibly rich

sweets? Am I being simply
disrespectful? What

of it? Glaciers melt and, yes,
this autumn is hotter than summer. So

Capitalism won; the cadres swapped
their gray Mao-esque suits

for the latest Armani. Indeed
your ennui and my disenchantment

match. We're in love, two ex-pats
struggling to finish our moon-cakes

in the furnace of 'the next Shanghai'.

The Traitor

We wept and cleared the land
of their barbwires and bombs.

Their calloused victims
we cheered with our victory.

The ruins of invasion
we set to reconstruct with

the songs of resurrection
tingling our moistened lips.

Reconciliation? That too.
And retribution

we sought from the ousted.
How our children

rejoiced at the ecstasy
of our revival. But did they

laugh with joyfulness
or snigger with mischief

and unconscious fear? We
should have granted

closer attention to the
expressions of our 'hopeful'. We

busied with the tasks
of intrepid restoration

and justice. 'Revenge'
we forbade as a word

but in action? Traitors
we indoctrinated in sedition

and punished in public. The nooses
rarely free of the necks

of vicious collaborators. And
our early songs of hope

now lumbering overtures
of nationalism and grievance. Did

our leaders succumb
to mere temptations of might

or something altogether
more terrible, as the piles

of dead 'traitors' mounted
higher than our reclaimed and revised

national landmarks? Our flag
the embodiment of all

our heritage, our religion, our pride
and other mythic colours

flapped higher than our leaders'
intrigue and rivalry. Then

the war with barbarian neighbours. I
enlisted to fight for our freedom

to be entrapped in a charred trench
for weeks, months, years. The reek

of my comrades' cadavers
rotted my nose; the sight of their

decomposition ... how
I began to snigger with horror

like the children who now
brutalised by the coarse notes

of our symphonic national anthem
marched and brandished guns

beneath the cutthroat and vehement
sneer of our Supreme Revolutionary

Leader. They declared me
unfit. I agreed wholeheartedly

with their dangerous verdict. They
replaced me with a less sentimental

freedom-fighter. Delirious
with what I'd seen in the battle

and naturally haunted by the face
of the 'elitist' 'counter-revolutionary'

I myself had hanged
during the early years of Liberation,

I spat at our national flag
and farted with all my intestinal vigour

during the national anthem. They
shaved my head, branded me names

that I finally found incomprehensible
and, though left to survive

unlike so, so many others
the blisters of the word 'traitor'

still sting my flesh, so many years
since the Revolution ended.

Immigration

I'll tell you why.
To survive

the onslaught of religion.
To outlive

the ghosts of martyrs.
To recover

from the world's longest war
since WWII. To live

beyond the hatreds
of patriotism. To see

the kinder face of humanity.
To think

free of the Faith's manacles.
To believe

without the obligation
of forming belief.

To discover
the basic joys of being.

The price? I'll tell you.
Evaporation.

Marginalised to the point
of disappearance.

Barred for nothing
more profound than a shade

of skin, a tone
of speech, a taste

of lifestyle. Alienated
beyond the word.

Ignored by the mighty.
Detested by the commoner.

Worth it? Doubtless.
To finally grasp

humanity's fraudulent truth.
To dream

the sweetness of equality.
To see past

the façade of brotherhood.
To be touched

you might say, by the rays
of a luminous discovery.

To abandon
all faith, and come to cherish

the immense solitude
of non-believing.

To desire. To know
the power of desire. To wait

joyfully amid unpalatable sadness.
Recommend it?

Only to loathsome enemies
and to my dearest friends.

The Honest Truth

For Penny

Everything is beautiful. Flowers
grin from the gutters where

no rain-soaked pages
of worn-out porno magazines, no

plastic bottles, no junk-food wrapping
sting the eye. And no,

I was perfectly happy
before I met you. Everything

is perfect. Television is not
the devil's instrument; it does not

manipulate; it does not cast a spell
of pathological consumerism

over the masses. At any rate, the masses
prefer companionship and poetry.

No, they do no not deify
adolescent football players. And no,

I was not disillusioned
with life before I met you. No one

is disillusioned. We're not
heading for a new Dark Ages. World leaders,

the US president in particular, are not
in the business of war. They

are the servants of democracy,
dedicated to working for the people

not only for the financial giants.
And no, I did not

find it impossible to smile
before I met you: the world

is filled with smiles. There are no
swastikas painted on Jewish graves; no

Muslim migrants bludgeoned to death
by skinheads; no Arab teenagers

blowing themselves up in pizza shops; no
Russian tanks levelling

villages; and no American soldiers
killing their prisoners

in macabre sex acts. And no,
it's not because of you

that I haven't merged with my repulsion.
It's not because of you

that I can hold on to my humanity
in this beautiful, perfect and smiling

world.

Embers

Rumi

I escaped from the city
barefooted. I escaped from the fires

naked, except for the bag
of ancient books

slung over my back.
I ran into the desert. The horsemen

chased. Their torches
had coloured the tenements.

I ran for months. Finally
on a glorious night

I stopped. The raiders had given up
on me. I was alone

with the moon and the sand-dunes.
I looked down at my feet.

They were skinned.
I looked at my trace: red footprints

dark on the glowing plain.
I thought about my tribe

butchered as sacrificial beasts.
I remembered their smiles

before the flames. On the holy night
I knelt before the moon

and wept. In the desert
tears are elixir. From their pool

a fountain bubbled. I cleaned my scars
in the water. The books

weighed on my body. I took them out
and one by one

dipped them into the spring.
All knowledge, all art, and all history

drowned before my eyes. Freed
from the clutch of paper

words' ink dissolved in the lake.
I then drank. I was saved.

Three Quatrains by Rumi

From Persian

    I.

Since your face is the Idol, idolatry is better.
Since the Wine comes from your Chalice, drunkenness is better.

I was annihilated in the being of your Love.
Compared to one thousand beings, this Nothingness is better.

    II.

You won't be lonely if you don't fear me
and your shop will prosper from this commerce.

Don't fear the night if you seek moon's face;
take the thorns, and you'll know the fragrance.

    III.

With Matt Hetherington

I want your Love to raise me out of life
and from your sea to rise beyond both worlds.

I need your sun for rain to come
since you're the one who raises mist up from the sea.

A Ghazal by Rumi

From Persian, with Matt Hetherington

Either I teach you faithfulness
      or learn faithlessness from you.

Either I teach you patience
      or learn ridicule from you.

And from which of our prayers
      will I learn praise for you?

Reveal yourself, so nations
      learn enlightenment from you.

For until ridicule leaves this world
      I'll learn only deceit from you.

Beaten

My vanguard routed
by their grinning gatekeepers,

my artillery annulled
by their agile trebuchets

I watch the defeat from
a crumbling keep before

abandoning my sinking
battalions, my nostrils filled

with the fumes of fear,
and head pummelled by

the cries of dying friends.
Back to devising strategy?

No. My offence utterly
dissolved by their categorical

force — a farce really, compared
to the might of their impeding

assault. You follow the militaristic
metaphors? Try this: my plants

die in the meanness of
their soil, the burgeoning leaves

droop in the absence of light
and whatever fruit survives

the harshness of birth
rots on the ignored shelves. I'll

try again: the Beloved,
so impossible to love. Her face

shows no awareness of
my roses and hand-crafted gifts.

Her heart remains
captured by the uncanny guile

of liars and thieves. She
doesn't even flirt with us

anymore. But enough
clichés. You get

the picture. Let's put
the images to motion and have

a sense of narrative. After
escaping from the ruins

of defeat, with hopes
of fecundity festering

in the furrows of waste,
with my Beloved

blushing in another's bed
do I contemplate licking

wounds? Mending (to stick to
clichés) my broken heart?

I repeat: my tongue
is the very thing that was

crushed. My heart never
had the chance to form. Idiom

doesn't suffice. Fertility
a truly awful metaphor. Instead

I'll rephrase: my campaign
never one of conquest, harvest

or even love. My armies
never positioned to charge

the foe's impenetrable citadels. She
never imagined me as

an equal. Why bother then
with an association of fables?

So the brutal admission:
I was always an inferior

spat upon by the lovely. My war
never an expansion

but basic rebellion. Famine
a much more apt word

for the condition of my life
than farm or garden. Victory

a false fantasy and survival
the only exigency. You see

resistance, not romance
beats at the heart of my being.

I speak to penetrate
the impositions of silence. I can't

even begin to seduce
the listener. I must protect

my buds amid the locust
and not turn fruit into a fetish.

The desire was never
to win but to last

and remain human amid
this savagery. Integrity

was the prize, not victory. Am I
so utterly defeated

to valorise failure? No doubt
but also adroit: the tale

of dispossession appeals more
than ambition. A struggle

to survive tyranny more righteous
than a thirst for sex,

juicy fruits and success. The truth
of defeat alludes

and hurts beyond argument; but
what follows depends

on the reality of imagination. Life
only continues as such.

Annihilation

Their whirling and the spinning
of their Fez and the skirts

of their pallid robes in tune
with the lascivious beating of drums

no doubt an exotic attraction
for bored modern viewers. But I'm

more than entertained by the dance
of Turkish dervishes and the rousing

mantras of Sufi masters, as I've veered
towards a crash with the ego. Did I

want this confrontation of 'base self'
and 'higher soul'? Sufi doctrines

always seemed archaic and, at best,
ornamental. Transcendentalism

put off this agnostic. The fantasy
comprised peace and sympathy. But the defeats

outweighed. Don't dismiss my complaint
as just that; don't confuse an admission

for grievance. I accept, as Césaire did,
the darkness of my physique: the colour

of my culture, the burden of my accent,
the barbarity of my politics and the certainty

of war. I dare say I'm at ease
with being your hated enemy. But the fantasy

foments further attempts at an armistice
and fraternity. How I've struggled

to be heard by you. How
dramatic my failure. So I'm more than

interested in the dervishes' desire
to annihilate an ego so embattled

it's a wounded fiend that makes the Minotaur
look like a Muppet. Don't be dull

by noting the hyperbole. What do you
care for my poetic license? Your powers

never granted me one. I've been so
caged in the labyrinth of conflict and deceit

that, again, the monster of my self
could rout Minotaur, Manticore and Medusa

with one lacklustre blow. And it would
take more than a vainglorious mythic hero

to slay these terrors. Do believe me, for I've
truly tried. Now I sit at the dusty shrines

of Sufi poets, utterly defeated and in love
with annihilation. My pride's perdition

rests with whirling like a millstone to turn
base metal into gold. No, this has

nothing to do with Jungian claptrap; not
at all an interpretation of the fantasy but

its sacred obliteration. The Sufis say
there are Seven Valleys of Love

and to dissolve as a drop in the ocean
of creation is the aim. They spin

dizzyingly to distort their senses and
forget their selves. Call it self-harm

and suicidal; but it may yet be
the Path of surviving your world of war.

A Ghazal by Attar

From Persian, with Ken Avery

Since there is no one to be our companion in Love
    the prayer-mat is for the pious; wine-dregs and vice for us.

A place where people's lives are twisted and divined by runes
    is not a place for rogues; so what's that got to do with us?

If the wine-bringers of the intellect sit with the devout
    their wine is for the ascetics; lees and hangovers for us.

Cure is for the purists, consternation for the broken,
    joyfulness for the do-gooders; while grief remembers us.

O pretender, you are not here to witness our wealth
    as the Beloved extorted all that we owned within us.

Vibrant words arrived from the messenger of truth:
    O weary, as you make your way, shed your grief for us.

Attar was drowned in sorrow along this Path.
    Because he's absolutely finished, his solace is with us.

Writer in Prison

Your cell is a cavern; the guards
grinding teeth outside your grotto

marginally refined ape-men; you
the last human in the world

of triumphant beasts. Is your pen
the key to emancipation?

No. The lock has no keyhole
and welded beyond breakage,

bolstered by all the energy
invested in orchestrating

your captivity. Such formality
staged for the incarceration

of one soul. The vilification,
the public outrage, the trial

and the theatrical castigation
all to ensure that the curtain

forever falls over your life. What
could a pen possibly do

to alter the absolute plot
of the script of so-called justice?

Zilch. Your freedom is untenable.
Barbarity always possesses

the upper hand. Don't waste
your vital ink doodling tears.

In your pre- or post- historic cave
you are the insider archaeologist.

Your pen is a shovel, chisel
and brush only for exhuming

the bruised icons, recovering the abject
tales and treasures from beneath

the stone, lava, rubble and sand
of the storms of tyranny. Please

don't get sentimental now.
You, writer in prison,

may yet be our saviour.

Iran

I cringe (or is it shiver?)
every time I hear the word

motherland. I'd like to think
my blatant internationalism

foments the reaction. But is it
the latent fear forever held

by you, my *pays natal*, the terror
of *un retour*? I'd like to

remember the scent of your
jasmine, the ooze of

your pomegranate's juice. But
the torture in your prisons

the sadism in your leaders' eyes
pervade the reminiscence. I'm

drawn to the romance
of your poets, memorialised

so lyrically in the sepulchral shrines
of Shiraz. The tales of turbaned

bards drinking the forbidden,
singing the heady praises of Love

fill me with the desire
to love you, but the ubiquity

of sub-machine guns,
the vigilance of the Guards

repel. And I've been repulsed
across the globe. I've been

made thoroughly homeless. Blame
Islam? The historical disaster

of a revolution without vision?
Anti-colonialism without

the aim of ending the slavery
of the soul to the superiority

of belief? Or, as always, 'them':
the Americans, greased up

for devouring your oil? Blame?
No, I'm not at all interested

in constructivism. I'll accuse,
as they say in my surrogate *patrie*,

'until the cows come home'. Why
the pretentious reliance on

Italicised French words and Anglo
slang? My mother-tongue

also terrifies. Once the language of
no doubt sublime poets and *ghazals*;

the discourse of submission
and hatred during my childhood.

Remember your theologians
interpreting reality? I don't want to.

I don't know if my psyche
can handle many more nightmares.

Let it suffice that I can recall
the purges, the bruises, the glow

of the incinerations. I'll have
you know that I now fathom what

you had in mind for me: a plot
among the 'martyrs'

in the Heaven of Zahra
mausoleum in Tehran. Now

I hear you're armed
to the teeth to continue your

infernal war against
timeless nemeses. Your wealthy

still holiday in Europe and plan
cosmetic surgeries. Your clerics

still issue death warrants
against 'apostates' and 'infidels'. I'm

almost dead in the quicksand
of the deserts of foreignness and

exile. Do I even begin to dare
contemplate a return

to the makeshift terrains
of memory? To the localities

that cultivated my senses
of placement, to the orchards

that I wandered as a bored
child? The people are mostly dead.

The remaining form a diaspora
of regret and disillusionment. I'm,

as I said, not a positivist. Only
a fickle and shuddering ghost

rejuvenated and alarmed
by the mention of the word

motherland.

Eyes in Times of War

After Adom Yarjanian

I.

Gouging them out, no matter
how violently, so very feeble

when what's passed through
burns beyond the lens. The embers

of reality hoarded in the kiln
of experience, this palimpsest

of seething and seeing the ablaze
sites. One: the classmate

who extolled the drama of
jihad as I cringed. His, no doubt

the dull repetition of the ethos
propagated by the wartime regime

of my birthplace, and the blasts
of so many boy-martyrs at the Front.

Dire conviction? How should I
forget the zeal of his eyes? By

jabbing mine with a needle
to expunge the images of

our carrions, the footage of
charred heroes? But it's the mind,

the repository of all grotesquerie.
And the adroit eyes played their

devious part. Another: the volunteer
Islamic Guard pointing AK47

at my face. The muzzle itself
just metal, but the heat of his

desire to kill so evocative
of my own incipient disgust. Am

I being oversensitive? You
call that rite-of-passage? Perhaps. But

here's another: a heroin-dealer
convulsing on the noose

suspended from a crane at
the intersection of our street and

Tehran's main highway. The grocery-
bag on his face almost comical

as his body writhed with full tragic
intensity. Say, how could I

forget that? Scratch out
the treacherous eyes that exploited

my teenager's curiosity?

II.

Never
mind. We did escape the *Grand*

Guignol of Iran. In times of war
people become theatrically

macabre. In Australia
foreign military invasion

has never ceased. The conquerors
know the indefensibility

of their victory. Two hundred
years of frontier massacres

and casual genocides can't
find closure in a mere wish for

an end. I saw the scars
on a boy's wrists. He'd just been

kicked out of a pub. He swore
he had a job, but the tone

of his skin betrayed the facts
on his resume. He also swore

he'd kill himself. We got drunk
and I later saw the cigarette burns

on his back. Would it suffice
for me to also stamp cigarettes

into my eyes to make the marks
of his mutilations fade? Didn't I see

a university classmate a day
before he walked in front of the train

between Gold Coast and
Brisbane? Have my eyes only

magnetised morbidity? He
didn't say much. I was frankly

annoyed by his sleeping
with a girl that I had a crush

on. I asked him about his
writing. He was on drugs. Did I

guess that he'd top himself
in a day? Then, the bubbly

ex-model who smiled in my
direction before way-faring

into the night. The flash
of her crescent mouth filled

with bright teeth and flanked
by cavernous dimples. Found

dead in the morning with foam
and blood coating her nostrils, her

full 'kissable' lips chapped
and blue, she was instantly

forgotten by the 'boys' who fed her
the dope before the orgy. Why

do I remember this and other
deaths? Why graze my eyes over

the fields of war and horror
in memory? Are these recollections

research for the impending atrocities
of terrorism, War on Terror, the Clash

of Civilisations, ecological
apocalypses, and the soul's destined

travesties and tragedies? Have I seen
nothing yet?

Angelus Novus

After Walter Benjamin

The angry wind has shorn the feathers
off his wings.

He levitates on a fixed spot
by the highway. Is the wind

caused by the flood
of the speeding vehicles

or indeed hurled
by the rabid gods of heaven?

The angel can't tell. He watches
the atoms of his wings' debris

twirl in the tempest. Why
with such affection? A longing

for what? For the ruins
no doubt; for what's been crushed

by the onslaught of the divine
tragedy. Can he save any of it

from irretrievable erasure?
Will his suitcase have room

enough for the volume
of such immeasurable loss?

He can't tell
as yet. He floats, resists

being swallowed by the storm
and doesn't hitch a lift.

Good Idea?

For Justin Clemens

Fin-de-Siècle France
much more congenial

to the glum exuberance
of your thoughts. Exile

in the land of mediocrity
and gum-trees, no doubt

unjust as Ovid's. Our Caesar
a banal bureaucrat who

jogs around a lake
in Canberra. 'Intellectuals'

debate base quackery
in our desert island's

bored media. Nearly
buried by the sandstorm's

insignificance, I asked
for a good idea. My thesis

a pauper's grave,
withered formulae; since

the thirst for life
often kills. I was, frankly,

serious. You: "Then again
there are no good ideas"

and discoursed
with obstinate, burning

exactitude the belief
of doubt. Abelard lost

his balls for this. You
may be the last cynic

in the barren domain
of odious and senseless

pastoral optimism;
the strained and resilient

rope flung toward
my hands sinking in

the sand of the island's
so-called culture, or lack

thereof. Amen.

Barfly

For Kris Terbutt

Nostalgia always displaces
the clout of memory

in the memoirs they forced
us to revere at university. So

do I still lyricise the past
when the present rattles

to the quakes of history? This
morning: *Barfly*; the only

show in English on
the Mandarin TV. I'm now

pummelled by the force
of reminiscence; your

favourite film. We talked
over bourbon before my shift

to China; but the Bukowski flick
incites. I must put to the page

what we might've already
blurted. Memories, in fact,

of so many wanderings along
the austere steppes of our

rites-of-passage. First, your stance
in the humdrum cemetery

and the babble of poetry. Such
an impression you made

in the wastes of Southport. Then
you moved and I endured

the improbability of talent
in a tourist town. I followed

you to where Australia
supposedly revokes its cringe

from the arts. Your hands full
with paintbrush and prosody

and mine chained to the load
of study. Again, I won't

allow nostalgia. Just facts. You
had girls and a gift

but lacked the patience
for wrapping it. Mine, if any,

soon irritated worse than
bad relationships. So many

of them. One hurled a saucepan
(coffee mug?) at your head; heir

to another who stalked. Mine
a certified manic before certain

boredoms. Did they touch
the surface of our curse? Well,

it's not my view, but
another fact. How else to term

this fixation? Snivel
the kitchen-hand blues for

anything other than
a genuine blight? You know

my anger: the racist
publishers, gutless teachers,

and the insipid masses. Yours
to do with the barbarity

of hospitality, the apathy
of the artless scenes. What

motivates our perseverance
with the utterly thankless?

The *Barfly* fantasy? Still
hoping to be 'discovered'?

By whom? At least love
has smoked us out. I'm

candidly happy with my
marriage. You have an

unflinching comrade. But
we continue with the quest

for what? Recognition
by the phoneys we can't ever

comprehend? The revival
of spiritual urges we had

thoroughly wringed out of us
by religions? Your pieces

are harsh and happy, mine
(I've been told) polemical. Our

persistence astounds. Did we
even stand a chance against

the romance of dirty, honest
realism? Can we ever rout

the vile gatekeepers? Am I
conscripted to the chalkboard,

at best, and you
to the demands of drunks

and the voracious? Well
so much for nostalgia. So much

has been omitted: the abusive
friends, the fickle mentors,

the glistening moments
of triumph like threads of silk

amid the coarse cloth
of our lives' tapestry. And

the movie. I admit
I'm looking forward to

its repeat on the only
English-language station. It

reminds why I've again
become an exile, as you

stretch and cover canvases
with immense skeletal flowers

and ghosts of martyred birds.

The Hermit

For Edward Said

He stands outside the walls
with a torch. To the courtiers

his light is a novelty; something quaint
flickering like a distant star

amusing, at best, but often
trivial and dismissible. He stands there

in the rain, in the midst of wars
his beard grows long and white

his torch burning night and day.
The empire's nobles and courtesans

occasionally remark on his perseverance
and almost always mock his passions. But

to us, the homeless peasants
his torch is an oracle

the beacon of survival
during the onslaughts of storm and pillage.

We gather around like moths
warm our eyes on his flames

thanking our goddesses and gods
that he's here to shed light

on our forgotten lives. O, how
lost we'll be without him.

This Thing

For/with Penny

How to begin to define it
this momentous thing

between us? A monosyllable
rhyming with 'dove'

and 'above', so dull
and dubiously religious

compared to the spirit
of our connection. Not that

talk of the numinous
wouldn't apply. Your penchant

for the Tarot, mine
for the Sufis, altogether

I suspect more transcendental
than the babble

of necessity and hope
desired by our former selves. Now

I can't say if 'love' ever
belonged to my former lexicon

of merely being
with someone. A confession?

That wouldn't become
my professed agnosticism; but

fate always the star
of your astrological ciphers

and my horoscope
no doubt a serendipity

in the house of your heart. Mine,
(forgive the war metaphors)

a fortress reigned by
the tyrant of solipsism until

your ram battered the gates
and your vanguard scaled

the ramparts. Now the untied
captives laze on the fields

of your victory. The tyrant
a cross between theologian

and troubadour, no longer a threat
to my peasants. But what

have you gained
from this conquest? Do I

make you happy? What do you call
this earth-shaking thing

between us? I suspect
your images altogether sharper

than my medievalist detours, say
animals—am I

salamander to your unicorn
or you a yellow crane

perched on my tortoise? Or
fairy tale: you see

yourself as a compassionate
Little Red Riding Hood

to my repentant wolf? Not
very likely. I've never really

queried eating you; but
you must've glanced

the dangers of sharing life
with a confused and brooding

loner. A person of your insight
doesn't mess around

in Blue Beard's chamber.
And I'm frankly just

a diffused dragon. So do we
call this thing

domestication? What about
the euphoria of escaping

our house together
and boarding planes? Am I

your accomplice
or live cargo? Does it sound

like complaint? It's in fact
a celebration of the ecstatic

thing between us. I ask you
to comment. You say:

"It's a magical
ever-changing intertwining

of two lives on levels
mundane and divine".

Golden Girl by R. Shiri

From Persian. Rahman Shiri was an Iranian asylum seeker. This poem was written during his mandatory imprisonment at Port Hedland detention centre, Australia. He has since been deported.

Golden girl
in this cell
you became a garden
prosperous
and in there, I rediscovered my dreams

You became a window
open and wide
and in there, I reclaimed my vision

You became a pulpit
facing the desert and the sun
and in there, I retrieved my life.

Golden girl
in this cell
my last sunset
was the time of your repose and mourning
although I know
they have set fire to the garden of your dreams
shut the windows of your eyes
planted thorns in the pulpit of your life
and you
are silent with sadness
burying me
with your dolls in the soil.

A Ghazal by Hafez

From Persian

Hey morning breeze, lover's tomb o where?
    Temple of her severed moon o where?

Tarnished night's lost heralds of hope.
    Site of our sainted meeting o where?

Birth bears marks of ruin and defeat.
    In the ruins ask the wise o where?

So prophets must battle for bravery.
    Keeper of divine secrets o where?

My hair entangles a thousand flames.
    Past sorrow, deliverance o where?

Ask then from the woman of dreams
    The core of my captivity, o where?

Mind rots in the absence of her glow
    Soul left the body, her brow o where?

Wine, songs and parties invite us but
    No bliss without love, lover o where?

Autumn's wind has ruined the old grass
    Don't waste time then; young flower o where?

My People

Snared by nostalgia
reduced to an absolute past

o my people
how shall I save you?

Your faces reduced to eyes
that flicker from the dark

oppression of forgetting.
How shall my remembering

have the means to oppose
the sublime tyranny of time?

How my treasures
are buried with your being

beneath the rubble of memory.
Your name is a whimper

a history reduced to a sigh
beneath the mess of earthquakes,

revolutions and wars.
Your ancient tongue an elegy

at the funeral of belonging.
No, I can't save you

but place, once in a while
my freshest rose at the mausoleum

of your name, o my family.
And as the phases of my loneliness

wane towards a dark moon
I shall erect memorials

for the songs of your fading eyes
in the lands of annihilation.

Retrospect

Teeth in Times of War (for 8 October 2001)

With Joe De Iacovo

They introduced a dental plan
the day Afghanistan got bombed
so I flicked my teeth with a fingernail
as the American Alliance carved
cavities into Kabul's ravines.

I plan to buy a new toothbrush
to change the shape of rot
to lie down watching jets cut
the sky into fang-shaped advertisements
showing-off the benefits of flouride.

If troops return, smeared
in goat herders' and messiahs' plaque,
gums tired of chewing on bombs
and smouldering bones,
the dental plan will be waiting

so heroes can smile on CNNN
and everybody will go . . . ahhhhhhhh!

The Ghosts (from *elixir: a story in poetry*)

Grandmother, never seen you this young
    without your usual hunch standing upright
        unveiled
        in a traditional purple and green
        Persian country folk dress that girls wear
        for the first thirteen days of spring
  Angel of Breeze
  air's hostess
      your lustrous face shines
      in paths of stars against the dark cave's backdrop

    Your eyes roar
        the tropic's might
a short distance away, watching over
the indigenous elder, with proud white beard
a shaman coloured with spots of red and white
    painted by his land's dreamy fingers
I see now, original H.S. owner of my instrument
    a poet I can tell, like Hafez   who
      isn't too grumpy about being conjured up
awake after all these centuries
the quiet bard with a quaint smile,
    Kindly pour into a Jewelled Chalice
    Jaam-e Jahan
    Cup of World
        drink of life
        from the small lake
        circled by rocks
    where children and others of the tribe
    used to drink from
        before

                    they came and stole the child from his kin
                    and gave him to a family in the City,
years later his lover blessed him with the Pen.
So he became a Poet.
                    And Hafez of Shiraz, the bard
                    your elegant long fingers grasp
                    magician's potion against my eyes.
I can't absorb your cup's intricate adornments in the darkness
                    but I smell
                    the sedative seduction of its liquid.
Now I become.
                    Grant the engraved goblet to her
                    My wine-bringer Goddess
                    Angel, host me the Wine

                                        So that we wet
                    our lips,
and on the Walls of our Cave
                    I Carve
                    with the Pen's tip
                    ready to cut
                    and release the poetry
                    of confession
                    and the alphabet
                    of absolution
                    so that I unlock the coffers of language
                    so that I'll print freedom
                    on the pages of life's prison.

ABC (from *elixir: a story in poetry*)

Persia, which most people call Iran,
on the stretch between Arabia and India
    twenty-something years ago

        Mum shrieked with my birth
in a moderate yet modernised hospital
      and outside, the Islamic Revolution
engulfed my parents' ephemeral mirth
        fanatics shouting and frantically burning
pictures of our toppled king and his regalia
    in the late 70s.

    It was all an incomprehensible religious/political thing to me
'cos an American kids' show
    diverted my curiosity from my uncle's smoking bullet wound
to an actor in a yellow feathery bird's costume on the box
saying: "**A** for **a**pple"
        the naïve imperialist Big Bird
couldn't teach me English 'cos more resonant than his singalong
      A was for Allah   Islam's God.
Ernie's **B** for **b**anana
        was overshadowed by **B** of ***b****allah*:
        Persian for disaster
as a religious rebel's rock smashed our dining room window
    and Sesame Street was axed and replaced by the telecast
      of names and photos of closed-eyed corpses
of the Peacock Throne's ministers and generals
    executed by Muslim revolutionaries.
    Mum blocked my eyes
as the corrupt and whimsical Shah
    nervously boarded a French aeroplane
to flee from the enraged militant victors.

So began the Islamic Republic of Iran and Mum
    at the point of misogyny's machine-guns
veiled her hair with an enforced grey scarf
    that in time became a black tent
by the Ayatollah's draconian ordinance.

With thick eyebrows and a robust white beard
old Ayatollah announced: "Veil is morality's consolation"
    but in women's covered figures I saw sexuality's condemnation
as the illiterate thugs of 'Hezb-Allah' (Allah's Sect) poured fuel
    over the heaps of literature, film and paintings
proud to be 'anti-art', the macho rednecks claimed:
    "We are delivering the people from a corrupting culture"
I saw my uncles grieve over our diminishing heritage.
In the aftermath of book-burnings libraries became sports centres
and physical competition replaced Persia's poetic aspirations
as in the first week of my single-sex school
    the principal seized my doodles and caricatures
shredded them in front of the class and shouted: "Art
    is unpatriotic, useless and un-Islamic"
signalling to the bigger boys to drag me
    over the asphalt playground
with shaved head
    on the pain of being kicked and spat on
I was picked for a football team.

Education was a matter of endurance
trying to ignore the Pen's temptation
I did my best to absorb the Koran, to enjoy football
but I couldn't help wondering about the reason
behind us being blatantly dumbed down
by the school's regime of sport and religion

until it all fell into its sadistic pattern
when the teacher's chalk drew on the board
the word *Jihad* — Arabic for fighting
on the day war
with Iraq broke out
    legions of sporty men and religious women
    marched and shouted:
        "There is no God but Allah!
                We'll kill for Him!
        There is no God but Allah!
                Death to Saddam!"
But in my vocabulary **G** and **H** signified

    guns (AK47s, UZs, etc)
followed by the **h**orror
of abruptly dying
when Iraqi jets screeched through our city's sky
        and dropped an average of 5 bombs
    every week
        for at least a quarter of the 8 year war.
My estimate:
    52 (weeks per year)
times
    5 (bombs)   =   260
times
    20 (civilians killed by each bomb — on average)
        =   5,200
times
    2 (¼ of 8 years)
        =   10,400
        people killed in our city alone
    by Saddam's hi-tech Western bombs. But

once in the bomb-shelter
as families thawed from the macabre stillness of
'lucky it wasn't us tonight but what about tomorrow night?'
My grandmother, *Maadar Joon*
      sensed me fidgeting with anxiety or perhaps
she felt pity for a child growing up during
      the Century's longest war since the Second World War
I was 8 or 9 when she smiled and granted: "Here, my son;
      My old pen. Show me your writing later."
She had been one of Iran's first literate women and one
      with famous handwriting and a supreme memory
for mystical verse. After her death, I was told
      that when younger, she'd joined an Order of Sufis
and roamed the plains of central Iran barefooted
      chanting the poems of Hafiz and Rumi for months
with a flask of water, rosary beads and no food.

During the 80s, as my childhood passed:

    I   was for **I**slam as well as **i**gnorance

    J   was for **J**ihad as well as **j**ailhouse
             (an unspecified number of Iranian dissenters—
             thousands—unofficially executed by the Islamic
             regime)

    K   for **K**oran as well as **k**illing
             (During the 8 year was with Iraq just under a
             million Iranians—soldiers and civilians—killed by
             Saddam)

L   for my Dad's **luck**
            when his visa was finally approved

M   for '**me**' and '**my**' abandoned identity
            also for **Malaysia** — our week-long stop before

N   for **Ned** Kelly
            the only thing I'd read about Australia
            before migrating to 'the Lucky Country'
            at the age of 14
            in the early 90s.

            O my...
                     Crossed my mind and formed on my lips
            when I saw my first unveiled woman
                 welcoming the passengers at the airport.
            I'd never known
                the magic of a woman's curls or an
unabashed smile. Also
"**O**" the cabdriver said, driving us to a hotel
     "This is a bloody marvellous country!"
Puberty crept just as dad planned
     our future in the land of gum trees and grinning receptionists
he enrolled me in a **p**ublic high school
without worrying that I didn't know a word or letter of English.

               But I still had my Grandmother's **P**en
                  and before school began
               I mimicked the writings of billboards and street signs
                   I wrote using the unfamiliar alphabet
               Qantas, **q**uarantine and **Q**ueensland
                    and practised saying 'hello' in the mirror

before my first day at school
I was intensely excited at the possibility
of being educated by modern and civilised teachers
having intelligent and compassionate peers
and
I felt blissful about sharing
classes and the playground with girls
of my own age who didn't hide their hair
who didn't get whipped for speaking to boys.

In the morning, in a uniform like the other kids,
with new haircut, pulled-up socks and my 'hello' rehearsed
I wandered about the playground before our first class

Scouring for someone, preferably a girl
to greet, smile and teach me to flirt and dance

I noticed the other students had silenced to stare
with an unusual apathy in their glance.

I exhumed the biggest smile I could muster
when a fat boy with scabbed face
in 'Screaming Jets' T-shirt and sports shorts
shouted from a distance:

"Camel-fucker"

I stopped smiling
without understanding what the bully had just yelled
to my disappointment, I had detected
the ignorance, the ugliness and the malice

of Iran's Islamic fundamentalists in the fundamentalist racist's voice.

    Another boy shouted: "You can't speak English, can ya,
                                                        fuckin' immigrant"

And another: "Fuck off. This isn't yer country."

So my hopes of making friends subsided
but I wasn't really worried until I realised
that the girls were laughing at me
                in solidarity with my new enemies.

    On the second day of school I was attacked
in front of an approving Physical Education teacher
beaten, lifted and dragged to a creek.
The bullies threw me off a small bridge and ran off.
My ears filled with water and the sport teacher's order:

                "Tell your fuckin' Arab mates to fuck off.
                We don't like darkies in Australia.
                We don't like fuckin' Muslims in Queensland.
                Tell your parents to fuck off, alright
                or we'll blow up your fuckin' mosques."

The next day, when my mother complained to the principal
he laughed at her phrasing when she said
        "Arash beaten very much and teacher encourage this!"
He corrected her and said: "Look,
      boys will be boys. Now, your son
      has to learn to stand up for himself. Life must've been
      pretty easygoing where you lot came from.
      He mustn't be used to a bit of rough-and-tumble, eh?

Where was it again? Iraq? India?
Look, Australia is a tough place. What I'm saying is
he can't be a mummy's boy forever now, can he?"

Maybe if I'd known of Australia's history of ethnic persecution
I would have stayed in Iran and coped with the familiar oppression.

If I'd known that a quarter of a million indigenous Australians
were massacred by Anglo-Celtic invaders during colonisation

that the invaders decreed laws that allowed stealing babies
from Aboriginal families for the purpose of racial 'purification'

if I'd known that entrance to non-'Whites' had been prohibited
for decades as an official policy of the flimsy and insecure federation

if I'd known that I'd be called an 'ethnic' (at best) and made an outcast,
if I'd known about Jimmy Governor and Pauline Hanson's 'One Nation'

I would've thought twice about a pointless life of recurrent alienation.

>   R   was for **r**ugby, **r**ock music and **r**um for others
>   **r**acism and **r**ejection by girls for me
>
>   S   for **s**ex, **s**urf and **s**and for others
>   **s**olitude and **s**uicide attempts for me
>
>   T   for **t**eams, **t**estosterone and **t**ests
>   and **t**rauma and the **t**rip
>   that changed my life at 18.

I had finished school and in the first year of university
finally made a friend, Felix;
he was cool, with dreadlocks and a guitar,
who took me to a pub and after a round of drinks
gave me my first acid trip and that night
I spoke to girls with unprecedented confidence
and a month later
I had sex
and moved out of home to live
with other uni students
to drink, take drugs and complain about life.

We failed every subject in the first semester and got arrested
      for urinating on an Anzac memorial
undermining our lecturers with sarcasm and cynicism
      we decided to stop going to lectures altogether
until in a drunk moment I received a call from Mum
who said Grandmother, *Maadar Joon*, had died in Iran.

I searched through my things and found her Pen
and deciding that I had learnt enough English
I thought about writing a poem. But nothing came
just lines crossed out by other lines
      on an otherwise blank page.

I went to a pub to wash off my failure with a beer or two.
It was quiet and I quickly downed successive drinks
when in the corner of my eye
      stood one of the high school bullies hunched over a beer.
I walked up and all I can remember before my automatic attack
is him turning around, sneering:
"It's you camel fucker ... long time no see."

Violence is not a cause for pride
            but sending the enemy to hospital
(with smashed face and crushed ribs)
satisfied the urges of vengeance
            with a validation of my competence.

I proudly spent the night at a police watch-house
with the Pen clenched in my bloody grip
            I asked one of the cops for some paper
and began to find my voice on the page.

After the court and community service
I was expelled from uni
for failing too many subjects and decided
to work and write poetry.

I worked as a kitchen-hand, delivery driver, door-to-door salesman
meeting the occasional woman at a bar or night-club
getting wasted and instead of making love
I could only wank between a pair of placid legs.

Love was a whimsical fantasy, a wish
beyond the scope of this beggar's wealth

until I met Jenny. She was working at a bookshop
and was surprised that a bum like me knew so much about books.

I was 20, she was 24
when we moved out of the City together
and rented a house in a hilly suburb
I told her: "I'm gonna immortalise you with my poetry, you'll see."

She said: "As long as we can pay the rent and buy food, OK?"

I agreed without realising the deception
    of commitment. Within weeks
I was drinking with other poets and getting booted
    from the workforce.

Jenny, beautiful, smart and honest
    changed and stopped sharing and encouraging
my ambitions in art and anarchy
when they sold the bookshop
    and replaced it with 'Sportsgirl'
she 'accidentally' lost my Grandmother's gift, the Pen
    at the post-office when paying a bill.
We began to argue and scream
    She called me an '**X**-generation layabout'
since instead of looking for work
    I watched trash like *Xena*
    and the *X-men* on the video
or ranted on about the King of Ancient Persia
    Xerxes.

We drifted apart and my attempt
    at reviving lust with an **X**-rated video
    flopped. She packed her bags.

        I wrote a drunken poem about her called 'You':

        "You have no preconception of my mad passion
        You have no perception of my life's mission

            Your desire equates my soul's confinement
            Your wishes serve my mind's retirement."

When she found it
she left.

That was two months before
I received a letter from Felix
    and decided to move back to the City.

        To end within retrospect
    life has been an alphabet of negation
            for every word heard or spoken
    I've believed and written the opposite.
        My fault or the world's?

Big Bird would have said
        "Z for zero" or "Z for zoo"
but I believe it's for the zenith
        of breaking the cages and the zeal
of my childhood hero Zorro
        or Persia's ancient prophet Zoroaster
who believed life was the field
        of constant battle between evil
and light.

A Memory

I'm not sure how old I was,
five or six.

All the lights out, pressing
cushions on my ears
to muffle the shockwaves.

Red siren and the coming
of a new batch of Iraqi jets.

I had the brave horses of the picture books
and a plastic figurine
my medieval mounted warrior
in pocket under the ping-pong table
in Grandmother's basement.
The first bomb's vibrations
clacked my bones.
I cringed my eyelids shut. I didn't wanna see.
The second one
felt like it was just down the road.

It rattled the table.
Adults froze in the omniscient fear.

I could feel it getting closer. I stuffed my ears with the cushions.
I didn't want to hear.
It's better not to see / hear it coming. It's better not to look.
I whispered to my knight—he seemed to agree.

The third bomb
landed on the opposite side of town
and the last two
ended up hitting an old hospital
many suburbs away from us.

Princess

I.

'Because she had the face of moonlight
and other girls squirmed with jealousy
    in her company
Because men forgot the battle and dropped their weapons
    at the mention of her name.'

A boy of six, I could do but ask
Grandmother the same question:

> He should've rode on back of his horse
> to the mountaintop where the White Fiend
> showered arrows and stones
> on the villages and cities below,
> Why did a girl, how could she
> distract him so?

Grandmother closed the thick tale of the book,
smiled at me, said:
'Because she had the face of moonlight.'

II.

The hero of the book trades his sword for business cards
as boy of six becomes man of twenty-three
and in place of book's brittle yellow pages there are
streets, pubs and offices, and newspapers printed
with phone numbers and job vacancies.
The White Fiend is now none other
than the liberal conservative politician in the parliament
or the same voice, the same typed letter

showering rejections, bills and new laws on the people below.
So with two university degrees and a finished manuscript
all I need is a war-horse

And it'll be a good day to fight,
                        a good day to die.

III.
         At the mention of her name
         All freezes, then returns again
         In a form neither liquid nor air.

IV.
She's Carlton's Princess of defiance and allure
whose green eyes are emerald, 'verd antique'
     to her, organs of sight are stones of enchantment
         around the large black pupils, often so immense
     they'll pull you in, under
         the talisman of lashes drawn out long from
her eyelids below the thin line of her darkly bowed brows
         they mesmerise against her fair skin
And when she smiles, the Princess
the subtle excitement of her scarlet lips
         incites heaven
this afternoon
she's wearing grey and black
to, perhaps,
         understate the magic.

V.

She's been juggling
pen with job and work around the house
losing appetite and sleep
and where's the time or the spirit to write
but her voice and her gestures
don't whine 'cos she's talking enthusiastically about
travel and university, and coffees
come slowly. We almost don't make it
to the movies in time, and it's raining outside
towards the bottle-shop after the film.
In the cab we're quiet, and since
I don't wanna come across as obvious
I stare out and not at her.
She's got the paper bag with our drinks on her lap
as the taxi crosses the river;

Princess has left Carlton
for the night.

VI.

In my room,
(I'm glad to have had it cleaned)
she looks at old photos on the wall
and I look at her tiny ponytail,
and the white neck, the celestial figure.
When she turns around and looks me straight
I feel dizzy, sit down and she
picks the music before

I have to tell her what would hurt
if kept a secret any more:

>The first time we met, months ago
>being new in town, another sorry excuse,
>I didn't think much, didn't try but to
>bargain for your affections,
>and when you turned away
>anger threw me towards another
>who asked me to burn the picture
>I'd drawn of you, and when I said no,
>the jealous bitch fed it to the fireplace
>herself... I missed my dreams of you,
>your voice rattling against my eardrums.
>When I saw you again I knew
>I'd rather be alone than to stay with her.

VII.

Princess listens, then tells
of her ex who would
make a very nice couple with mine:
>'He'd pressure me
>>to do things, some awful,
>
>I wasn't happy
>>and when people saw me they'd say:
>
>"Princess, you're not happy?
>You can't sleep?
>A pea under your pillow
>or a wolf howling
>within your heart?"'

VIII.

I think to tell her: I'd make you happy, no really, I would,
but her majestic gaze strips down my camouflage:
Princess, give me your hand to hold
She does, hesitantly.
Because there's nothing wrong with this world
but loneliness.
No enemy greater than loneliness
No crime worse than being alone.

IX.

Princess stays with me
Doesn't fly out the window on a magic rug
Doesn't deform at the stroke of midnight.

X.

In the first story ever written by men
the ancients called her Innana
Greeks named her Artemis, the Romans Diana
Tonight the Goddess of moon
     sits on the edge of my bed
and tells me about
     bra shopping, school and going to a party as a porn star
and when the moon hears her mellow voice
     and pales in her sturdy radiance
it squirms, too, in envy.

XI.

'What do you want from me?'
Princess asks, perhaps, understating her magic.

                        Closeness . . . sharing what I have of life
                        so far, with you, Princess . . .

XII.

With a soft look that shudders
the emeralds in her eye sockets:
'I've been through a lot
lately. Could you
wait?' I nod madly
I'm surprised my head doesn't fall off
and roll on the floor.

XIII.

Tomorrow I'll tell my publisher
to stick the fake contract up his arse
Tomorrow the White Fiend's slaying
will have to wait.
Tonight everything's perfect, no need to revolt,
when I sleep next to the Princess
with her insomnia, with my delusions of grandeur
all is perfect, all is fine
And there's no need to revolt, no need to fight
because she has a face of moonlight.

The Fruiting

There's an orange tree on top of a hill
its white blossoms are
like stars over the night-time crest
where moon is
the face of my beloved whose hair
is the ferns
shuffled by wind over a river
water moves
becomes the wetness of my eyes
when I praise
I become a butterfly swaying
around a candle
its light is the flame of a volcano
bright and orange
like the fruit
hanging from the lonesome tree
in the morning
on top of the hill.

Out of Water

For Penny

Moored in the lover's bay
my anchor's comfortably concealed

beneath her soft coral.
When the tides rise

her lighthouse signals home's trajectory
and I empty my treasures on her shores.

During the tranquil day
her clear playful wavelets

tickle my boats and tease the sand.
After decades of loss in the wild waters

I've finally reached the paradise
of her sacrosanct island.

Lover's Name

Your name
quakes the walls of my cell.
Syllables weaken the bricks,
sound eats out the cement
of life's solitary confinement.

Though you're a girl
material and flesh
your name's the cadence of myth
promising the divinity
of my ultimate deliverance.

Calling your name
is a hymn
disturbing the prison stones
and confusing the guards
by making the disenchanted dance.

You're the Sentinel

For Penny

You're the sentinel when I'm lost
    in the oceans of lonely excursion.

You're the clock when my sundial
    is shaded by the clouds of sadness.

You're the recipe that holds
    my mismatched ingredients together.

You're the dictionary that defines
    my dilapidated diction.

You're the street-directory
    that resolves my mind's traffic.

You're the light-switch that sheds off
    the darkness of solitude.

You're the timeless goddess
    who defies the truth of scepticism.

You're the brilliant witch
    who enchants my monastery.

You're the musician whose notes
    cure me of a lifelong deafness.

You're the drink that brings
    life to the drought of my lips.

Windows #3

I opened the windows and saw the giant flags
black and red, they had covered the winds
the tyranny of human symbols and arms
had mangled the air and veiled the sky.

Then I saw a bird, unspecific small bird
blue with yellow tail and clipped wings
tied to a flagpole with a tight metal string
its beak bound by grey masking tape.

It was too much for me, the oppression
I threw myself out the window and then
the bird caught the fire of my suicide
and flames raged up the firm flagpole.

And in the glory of freed wings
one by one the flags of the prison caught fire
and wind stormed again, sky was freed
the bird flew up to join the mating flocks.

I raised, shook off the blood and restarted the heart
and approached to open another window.

Printed in the United Kingdom
by Lightning Source UK Ltd.
112628UKS00001BA/8